DK SUPER Economics

SUPPLY and DEMAND

Explore the concepts of supply and demand and discover why some things are rare and others are everywhere

DK Learning

PRODUCED FOR DK BY
Editorial Just Content Limited
Design Studio Noel

Author Kimberly Wilson

Senior Editor Amelia Jones
Senior Art Editor Gilda Pacitti
Managing Editor Katherine Neep
Managing Art Editor Sarah Corcoran
Pre-Production Designer Rohit Singh
Production Controller Nancy-Jane Maun
Publisher Sarah Forbes
Managing Director, Learning Hilary Fine

First published in Great Britain in 2026 by
Dorling Kindersley Limited
20 Vauxhall Bridge Road,
London SW1V 2SA

The authorised representative in the EEA is
Dorling Kindersley Verlag GmbH. Arnulfstr. 124,
80636 Munich, Germany

Copyright © 2026 Dorling Kindersley Limited
A Penguin Random House Company
10 9 8 7 6 5 4 3 2 1
001–354563–Mar/2026

All rights reserved.
No part of this publication may be reproduced, stored in or
introduced into a retrieval system, or transmitted, in any form,
or by any means (electronic, mechanical, photocopying,
recording, or otherwise), without the prior written permission
of the copyright owner.
DK values and supports copyright. Thank you for respecting
intellectual property laws by not reproducing, scanning or
distributing any part of this publication by any means without
permission. By purchasing an authorised edition, you are
supporting writers and artists and enabling DK to continue
to publish books that inform and inspire readers.
No part of this publication may be used or reproduced in
any manner for the purpose of training artificial intelligence
technologies or systems. In accordance with Article 4(3)
of the DSM Directive 2019/790, DK expressly reserves this
work from the text and data mining exception.

A CIP catalogue record for this book
is available from the British Library.
ISBN: 978-0-2417-7442-7

Printed and bound in China

www.dk.com

This book was made with Forest Stewardship Council™ certified paper – one small step in DK's commitment to a sustainable future.
Learn more at www.dk.com/uk/information/sustainability

Contents

What Is Supply and Demand?	4
Producers and Sellers	6
Market Monopolies	8
Business Competition	10
Focus and Specialisation	12
Consumers and Buyers	14
Needs	16
Wants	18
Opportunity Costs	20
Benefits Big and Small	22
Tempting Incentives	24
Making a Profit	26
Following Trends	28
Surplus	30
Shortage	32
Economic Scarcity	34
Setting Goals	36
Everyday Economics: The Housing Market	38
Let's Try It! Plan It, Price It, Profit!	40
Vocabulary Builder: Planning in Action	42
Glossary	44
Index	46

Words in **bold** are explained in the glossary on page 44.

What Is Supply AND DEMAND?

Supply is how much of a good or service is available, and **demand** is how much people want it. Together, they affect the price. A price is what people pay for a good or service. Price follows demand, so if demand goes up or down, so does the price.

Supply

When strawberries are in season, there are more available, which means the supply increases. If customers still want the same amount they usually buy, demand stays the same, and the price will go down. In winter, the supply goes down, and the berries must be **imported** from warmer places. Since the demand is still the same and it costs more to import them, the price goes up.

Demand

Let's say a new recipe goes viral on social media, and the main ingredient is blueberries. Demand is at an all-time high. If the supply stays the same, the price will increase. But if bananas steal the spotlight and become the new trend, the demand for blueberries might go down. The farmers still grow the same amount, so the price should go down.

Graphing both supply and demand in a chart makes it easier to determine the **equilibrium**, where the two intersect. The equilibrium is the price when supply equals demand.

Think about it

Have you ever wanted something that suddenly became really popular – like a toy or snack – and noticed the price went up or it was sold out? Next time you shop, try to spot how prices change when more people want the same thing.

Producers and SELLERS

Together, producers and retailers supply goods and services to **consumers**. To create the goods, producers use **natural resources**, **human resources** and **capital resources**. Once products or services are ready, sellers offer them to consumers in markets, shops or online. While sellers focus on getting the products in the hands of consumers, producers concentrate on making them.

Producers

USING DIFFERENT RESOURCES
Farmers use natural resources, such as land and water, to grow food for us to eat. They also use machines like tractors, which are capital resources. The people who work on the farm are human resources.

PRODUCERS WHO ALSO SELL
A producer can also be the seller of their own products, for example a baker who makes bread and sells it in their bakery, or a carpenter who makes and sells furniture.

Sellers

THE WORLD'S BIGGEST SHOP CHAIN
In terms of **revenue**, the shop chain Walmart is the biggest seller in the world. It first opened in the US in 1962, but now it has stores all around the world selling food, clothes and electronics. It also sells goods online. People like shopping at Walmart because it is easy to find products and they are not too expensive.

SELLERS WHO ALSO MAKE PRODUCTS
Some companies, such as Lululemon and Gap Inc., manufacture, distribute and sell their products. This is called **vertical integration**. This way of operating helps efficiency, allows the company to control quality and keeps costs down.

Fascinating fact
With online shopping gaining popularity, companies like the manufacturer Proctor & Gamble have expanded from only producing to selling their products directly to customers.

Market MONOPOLIES

A **monopoly** is when one producer is the only company providing a product. This means there are no similar product choices available from anyone else. Because of this, the producer can use lower-quality or less expensive resources and charge a high price. They might not be motivated to explore ways to improve their product either.

Let's say you are the only gardener in town. Your customers do not have a choice but to come to you if they want their lawn mowed. That means you can charge whatever price you want. But if others start offering lawn mowing too, you might have to lower your price and offer edging and leaf blowing if you want to win business.

The UK government-owned British Gas Corporation had control of the national gas supply for a long time. Home and business customers received their gas from British Gas, which meant there were no competitors. In 1986, the government **privatised** British Gas, and later it was split into smaller companies to encourage competition and give consumers more choice.

Control and competition

In the late 1800s, Standard Oil controlled the oil pipelines in the United States and underpriced its product to cut out its competition, eventually becoming a monopoly. However, in 1890, the Sherman Antitrust Act was passed to prohibit unfair monopolies and encourage free competition. This led to Standard Oil breaking into several smaller companies.

De Beers is a company that mines and sells diamonds. It started in South Africa over 100 years ago. For a long time, De Beers controlled most of the world's diamonds. Today, De Beers is still a big diamond company, but it does not control the market like it used to.

Fascinating fact

An **oligopoly** is when a few companies control most of a market. This is not against the law, but they cannot work together to set prices or divide customers. An example of an oligopoly in the drinks industry is Coca-Cola and PepsiCo.

Business COMPETITION

Businesses must compete for consumers to choose their products. This encourages creativity and innovation in making higher-quality goods, giving people more choices and **competitive pricing**. These **benefits** of competition encourage people to make purchases, which also boosts the economy.

APPLE VS. SAMSUNG

Two of the biggest smartphone producers worldwide are Apple and Samsung. They compete by introducing new designs, faster speeds and improved cameras. This competitiveness gives consumers more choice and helps improve phone technology.

NIKE VS. ADIDAS

Nike and Adidas are two of the biggest sneaker brands. They make sports shoes and clothes for people around the world. Nike is known for its bold styles and strong advertising, while Adidas is famous for comfort and performance.

Fascinating fact

Kodak and Fujifilm were the leaders in the photography industry. With the rise of digital technology, Kodak continued to focus on film, while Fujifilm studied and followed the trend, becoming a **pioneer** in digital photography.

STARBUCKS VS. DUNKIN'

Starbucks and Dunkin' both focus on coffee as their main product, but each has found different ways to attract customers. Starbucks has coffee shops in more countries around the world and offers a big selection of drinks. The simpler menu and affordable prices at Dunkin' make it a popular choice for people who want fast options without spending too much.

Focus and SPECIALISATION

When people focus on a specific job or product rather than on several, they become more skilled and knowledgeable in that area. This is called **specialisation** and it helps improve efficiency, **productivity** and quality. Because specialised workers can produce more and waste less, it can reduce the cost of making the product. When production costs go down, prices for consumers often go down too.

This photograph shows a specially trained operator entering a programme into a machine. The machine then follows the instructions to make the part exactly right. This helps factories work faster and make fewer mistakes.

Instead of putting together an entire product, workers in manufacturing specialise in a job along an assembly line. For example, in a car factory, each part is put together in order along the way. This picture shows a row of newly manufactured car engines in a factory.

Fascinating fact

Crocs is an example of a company that specialises in their lightweight foam, odour-resistant shoes. Since launching in 2002, they have expanded into over 90 countries and sold over 600 million pairs!

There are many services that have opportunities to specialise. For example, doctors have more than 135 specialities, including **dermatology, cardiology, paediatrics** and surgery. Artists can specialise in oil painting, sculpting, digital art, photography or other areas.

Companies can also specialise in specific goods. Let's say you own a company that makes a variety of healthy foods. Your oat breakfast cookies are the most popular, so you decide to focus all of your time, energy and resources on those and to get rid of your less popular items.

Consumers and BUYERS

A consumer is someone who uses a good or service. The person who makes the purchase is the **buyer**. For example, when a parent purchases a toy for a child, the parent is the buyer, and the child who will be playing with it is the consumer. A lot of the time, the buyer and consumer are the same person.

Consumers

WHAT CONSUMERS CHOOSE
In an economy, consumers determine the demand for products. Their decisions can be based on many things, like the season or where they live. People do not buy as many beach towels in cold winters, and woolly hats are not on the shopping list during the hot summer months.

WHY PRICE MATTERS TO CONSUMERS
Income, price and value also influence people's purchasing. If the price is too high for someone to buy a product, they might wait until a sale. At the lower price, they might be able to afford the item, or they may feel like the purchase is worth it to them.

Buyers

BUYING WITH CONVENIENCE
If someone spots a hoodie they want online, and it arrives with 1-day free shipping, the convenience might be what convinces them to hit the "Buy" button.

WHAT INFLUENCES BUYERS
When friends or people on social media are all buying a specific product, there can be peer pressure added to the desire to buy something. Personal feelings and beliefs can also be a factor in decision-making.

Think about it

Most consumers read reviews when shopping and take them into account before they buy. What influences you when you are making purchasing decisions?

NEEDS

Needs are things a person must have to survive. Everyone has the same basic needs, but they might vary a little based on where they are in the world or how old they are. When making purchasing decisions, needs should always come first.

All people need water to maintain the right body temperature, carry nutrients and flush out waste. Those who live in hotter climates need more water to stay hydrated.

Food provides the nutrients and energy needed to survive. Depending on where you live, you might have different foods available. Near the coast, seafood might be a more common food. In rural areas near farms, fresh eggs might be part of daily diet.

Shelter is necessary, too, though the type depends on where you live. A tent might be sufficient shelter in warmer or drier climates, but in cooler regions thick walls and a solid roof are necessary.

Clothing is a necessity, but that also depends on the weather. A heavy coat is not needed in the desert, and a T-shirt and shorts are not enough to keep you warm in the **tundra**!

Think about it

What are some things you need every day to stay healthy, safe and comfortable?

WANTS

Things people buy that they do not need to survive are called **wants**. They usually make life easier or more enjoyable. Wants are limitless, but the ability to buy them all is not.

Clothes are a need, but wearing specific brand names and high fashion are wants.

Food is a need, but eating pasta at your favourite restaurant is a want.

When want increases for a good or service, demand increases. For example, when Taylor Swift tickets go on sale, lots of people want them. Because so many fans are trying to buy tickets, the demand goes up. That often increases the price, and sellers may release more tickets or add more shows to meet demand.

Let's say Fjällräven launches a new style in their backpack line. You see it advertised online, and friends at school start getting them. Now, you want one too, and you are not the only one. Consumers around the world all want their own and are willing to pay a higher price. As a result, if the company chooses to raise its price and produce more, it could make more money.

Fascinating fact

When people earn more, they can sometimes afford to buy luxury items they want, not need. These include products from designer brands like Louis Vuitton and Gucci. As demand rises, prices can go up. Some brands also raise prices to appear more special.

Opportunity COSTS

A cost is what someone gives in exchange for something else. For a consumer, the cost is usually money paid for a good or service. A company's costs include things like the materials to make a product, packaging, employee salaries, marketing and office space. Costs should be considered before making financial decisions.

An **opportunity cost** is the value of what is given up to get something else. For example, if you are at the beach with £5 and can only afford an ice cream cone or fudge, the one you do not choose is the opportunity cost.

It is important to think carefully before buying something – you can only use that money once, so you want to make the best choice.

Opportunity costs can also be in the future. If you choose to buy the souvenir you want today, you might not have money to buy the pool float you have been saving up for later.

Think about it

Have you ever bought something and later wished you had saved your money for something else? How did that make you feel? What would you do differently next time?

On the business side, companies also deal with trade-offs. For example, if a sports equipment brand chooses to focus on basketball gear instead of baseball items, it gives up the chance to earn money from baseball sales. The money they could have made from selling baseball equipment in the future is the opportunity cost.

Benefits Big AND SMALL

What a person or business gains from a choice they make is a benefit. For a consumer, the benefit from a purchase could be having what they bought. The product might make them happy or make their life easier. One of the biggest benefits for a business is making money.

If you save up and buy a ukulele, the benefit is having the new instrument. It could also be the way you feel about the purchase. Maybe you are proud because of all the chores and time it took to get it. Maybe having it means you can finally get music lessons.

A business benefit is the money made from selling the goods and services produced. When making decisions, the benefits should add up to more than the costs. You can figure this out by looking at the **benefit–cost ratio**.

Supermarket points cards offer a way for customers to save money. When you purchase items at the store, you earn points that become **discounts** later. This benefit motivates customers to continue shopping at the same store. The business also benefits because customers keep coming back.

Boosting sales

Incentives, such as free items, can encourage more people to buy. Even if there is a small added cost, businesses often use this strategy to increase overall profits. For example, imagine a food truck offers a free ice lolly (costing 50p) with each £10 meal. Sales rise from 20 to 30 meals, earning £300 instead of £200. The 30 ice lollies cost £15, but the extra £100 in sales means £85 more profit. The benefit–cost ratio is £85 to £15, making it a good deal.

Fascinating fact

Some costs and benefits cannot be measured. For example, some companies try to use recycled and organic materials. While the cost is clear, the benefit to the planet depends on what the company and its customers value.

Tempting INCENTIVES

Things that motivate people to do something are called incentives. Companies offer incentives to consumers, like special offers, rewards, free shipping, gifts with a purchase or a lower price than competitors. These offers make buying their products more **enticing** to customers.

Another incentive for consumers is income. When people earn enough money to afford a good or service, they are more likely to be motivated to make a purchase.

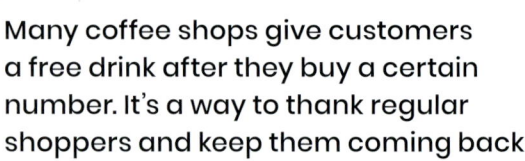

Many coffee shops give customers a free drink after they buy a certain number. It's a way to thank regular shoppers and keep them coming back.

Fascinating fact

Incentives can also be negative, like a company getting charged with fees for emissions and pollution they cause. This encourages a company to reduce pollution when producing goods.

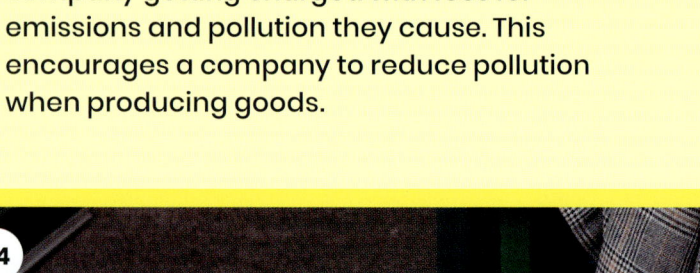

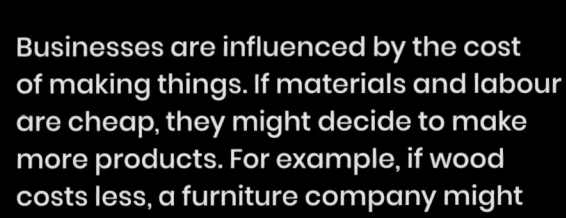

Businesses are influenced by the cost of making things. If materials and labour are cheap, they might decide to make more products. For example, if wood costs less, a furniture company might make more items.

Businesses might also receive tax or funding incentives from the government. This includes grant money for specific projects and tax credits, or deductions for doing things that benefit the environment, like using renewable energy.

Subsidies also give businesses financial incentives to stop production when there is a surplus. For example, if there is a surplus of wheat, farmers might receive money to reduce how much they grow.

25

Making A PROFIT

A profit is how much a company makes by selling its goods and services. To calculate profit, first you need to figure out **expenditure**. The expenditure includes all the costs of producing the good or service. This is then subtracted from the total money made from sales, also called revenue.

Fascinating fact

Some companies give away free apps or games but still make a profit. They earn money when users pay for extras like bonus levels, special tools or new features. This is called the **freemium** model.

Most popcorn manufacturers make about 15 to 30 pence in profit for every pound they earn. Some make even more. In places like cinemas, popcorn is even more profitable. A small bag of popcorn might cost the cinema less than 50 pence to make, but they can sell it for £3 or more. That means they keep most of the money as profit.

A designer pair of sunglasses might cost a company £15 to make, including materials, packaging, marketing and labour. When they sell them for £300, the profit is a whopping £285!

FROM SUPPLIES TO SALES

1 Let's say you are making and selling beaded keychains. The beads cost £8, the string is £3 and the metal rings are £2.

2 You spend £7 on card and markers to make signs to advertise and pay your sister £2 to hang the signs around your neighbourhood. All of this adds up to a total expenditure of £22.

3 With your supplies, you make 20 keyrings, and you decide to price them at £4 each.

4 When you sell out, your total revenue is £80. Minus the expenditure of £22, you make a £58 profit!

Following
TRENDS

Trends are patterns in how people spend money on goods and services. Trends are shaped by things like preferences, income and new technology. They can affect supply, demand and prices, and sometimes lead to new industries.

Fast fashion is a trend that focuses on creating new styles in mass quantities at lower prices rather than more expensive products. This makes fashion more accessible to people with different income levels. It creates a greater demand for affordable, trendy clothing, but it can also lead to overproduction and waste.

Social media made Dubai chocolate go viral. The bars were only available in the UAE, but consumers all over the world wanted them. This led other companies to start making their own versions. Many cost £10 or more each, while most other chocolate bars cost only a few pounds.

Brilliant branding

RoseArt, a school and art supply company, has followed trends several times. They did this when they met the demand for non-toxic crayons before competitors, and made licensing agreements to feature popular brands, like Barbie and Hot Wheels, on their back-to-school supplies.

More people are choosing products that are better for the environment. For example, some shops now let people buy refills of products to cut down on packaging. This trend helps reduce waste and protect nature.

Fascinating fact

The Dubai chocolate popularity also affected the supply chain. California, the world's number one exporter of pistachios, saw an immediate increase in demand.

SURPLUS

A surplus is when there is too much supply of a product combined with a drop in demand. In this case, shop shelves might be full of the product with even more stock in the stockroom. This can result in discounts or a **price reduction** to boost sales.

Sometimes, farmers in the US grow more corn than people and businesses need. When there is more corn than buyers demand, prices go down. Some of the corn may be stored or used for other things, like animal food or fuel. This photograph shows a big pile of corn that had to be stored outside because there was no more space indoors.

Between 2017 and 2020, the demand for organic milk increased, so prices did too. Suppliers met the demand by producing more. Then, with the growing popularity of plant-based milks, like almond, coconut and oat, the demand for organic cow's milk declined. This caused a surplus, and the price went down.

It can be hard for clothes shops to know exactly how much of each size and style to order. Weather can also affect what people want to buy. If it suddenly gets cold, customers may not want lightweight clothes like T-shirts or shorts. When this happens, shops may not sell all the items they ordered. The extra clothes that do not get sold become a surplus. Shops often have to put these items in the sale or send them to outlet shops to make room for new stock.

In 2022, a high demand and shortage of memory chips for smartphones and computers led companies to produce more. Once they did, demand did not stay where expected, resulting in a surplus.

Fascinating fact

Airline ticket prices often change because of supply and demand. If lots of seats on a flight are empty, airlines sometimes lower the price to get more people to book.

SHORTAGE

A shortage is the opposite of a surplus. It is when there is high demand for a product, and there is not enough for everyone who wants to buy it. Signs of a shortage, or **deficit**, are empty shelves in shops or price increases. Shortages are temporary and can be caused by an unexpected rise in demand or a decrease in supply.

When fidget spinners first came out, they were so popular that shops could not keep up with the high demand. Some companies even paid extra to fly shipments in instead of using slower methods, like ships or trucks. This helped get fidget spinners into stores more quickly, but it also made them more expensive for sellers due to the high cost of air freight.

The game of pickleball is another example. When it became very popular in the US, the demand for courts went up unexpectedly, and there were not enough available for everyone who wanted to play. With people competing for time slots, sports clubs converted tennis courts into pickleball courts to quickly meet demand.

Fascinating fact

Cocoa farms in Ghana and Côte d'Ivoire, the suppliers of half of the world's cocoa, experienced a loss of crops due to heatwaves from climate change in 2023 and 2024. A shortage resulted, and cocoa prices skyrocketed.

A shortage can also be caused by a lack of resources. The orange juice supply decreased when citrus greening disease took over orange groves in Brazil and Florida. Some farmers used expensive treatments to try and save the crops, others lost entire groves. Because the demand was still the same, this led to a surge in orange juice prices.

Economic SCARCITY

Imagine a new game is launched and you really want to buy it. When you go to the shop, there are none left. The number of people who want to buy the game is greater than the number available. Economists describe this as **scarcity**. Scarcity means that there is not enough of something for everyone to get what they want.

Structural scarcity means some people cannot get what they need because of a lack of **infrastructure**. Examples are access to clean water and enough food.

Fascinating fact

Diamonds are not as rare as people think. Diamond companies only release a small quantity. This makes them seem more special and valuable. This is called **artificial scarcity**.

SOLD OUT!

After the first *Toy Story* film was a big hit, around 2 million people wanted to buy a Buzz Lightyear figure. But the toy manufacturer had only made 50,000. Shops soon ran out. They became so difficult to find that some parents were willing to pay £100, four times the actual price of £25.

This is an example of **demand-driven** scarcity. It shows how things can become more valuable when there aren't enough to go around.

FROM BEAN TO BREW

A typical shop-bought jar of instant coffee might cost about £4. But some types cost much more. One example is a special – and unusual – coffee produced on a farm in Thailand.

1 First, the coffee farmers feed Asian elephants coffee cherries.

2 Then, they wait for the elephants to digest them. This takes between 12 and 72 hours.

3 When the elephants pass waste, the farmers take the digested coffee cherries out of the dung by hand.

4 Next, the farmers clean the coffee cherries.

5 After that, the beans are taken from inside the cherries. Then they are roasted and ready to be made into coffee!

1p £36

A regular cup of instant coffee costs about 1p, but a cup of Black Ivory coffee costs around £36. Black Ivory coffee is much more expensive because it takes a lot more time and effort to produce and can only be made in small quantities. This is an example of **supply-driven** scarcity.

When something is hard to find or takes a long time to produce, it often costs more money.

Setting GOALS

When a company sets goals, it analyses factors including past sales numbers, current trends and competitors. It will also look at whether people are spending money, the season, new technology and any supply issues. This research is called **demand forecasting**. Carefully considering these things can help a company set goals, manage inventory, increase profit and stay ahead of the competition.

1 Let's say a trainer company wants to improve sales and get an edge on the biggest competitors. The other companies are using 3D printing and new foam technology, but this company wants to offer something its competition does not have.

2 Since fitness apps are popular, the team researches making a smart trainer to track workout details. They soon discover there is a large supply of microchips and sensors available.

3 The festive season is coming up, so many people will purchase gifts. With the new year approaching, many will have fitness resolutions, too.

4 After looking at all the data, the company decides to roll out the new smart trainers to increase sales by 10 per cent.

5 To raise awareness and drive demand, the company launches a new website and a smart trainer advertising campaign.

Think about it

Many businesses are seasonal and plan production around when they expect to make the most sales. For example, swimsuit companies make the most sales in summer. What other types of businesses might plan around seasons?

Everyday ECONOMICS
The Housing Market

The law of supply and demand affects the housing market in the same way as products in other industries. Interest rates, the percentage a bank charges for loaning money, are a big incentive for home buyers, so they significantly impact the demand for housing. When interest rates are low, more people want to buy houses, because it costs them less.

A seller's market is when the demand for housing is high and more people want to buy than there are houses available. When supply is low like this, prices can go up. This can lead to a **housing boom**. Developers rush to build more homes during a boom while the demand is up.

If multiple people are trying to buy one house, there could be a bidding war, which means each person offers the most they are willing to pay for the home. This can drive the price of the house up even more, because people are competing for it.

If there are more houses on the market than people looking to buy, prices can go down. This is called a buyer's market. When the supply is really high, demand is really low and the prices drop drastically, it is called a **housing market crash**.

Most homes in the UK are put up for sale between March and May, when families start planning moves before the new school year. Homes often sell faster and for higher prices during this time.

What can you do?

Imagine a family is looking for a home to rent during a housing boom. Rents are rising fast, and flats are being taken quickly.

1. Draw a comic strip showing what happens as they search for their new home.
2. How do supply and demand affect their choices?

Let's TRY IT!

PLAN IT, PRICE IT, PROFIT!

Producers have to think carefully about how they use their time and materials to make products. In this activity, you will be a producer. Given a time limit, you will need to make decisions that will be most efficient and cost-effective, and that will make the most money.

You will need:
- Large container of dough or clay
- Paper
- Pencil
- Ruler
- Watch or timer

1 Get ready to make products out of dough! In this challenge a 2.5 cm ball is worth £1, a 12 cm snake is worth £3, and a coil is worth £4.

2 Set the timer for 3 minutes and start! Make sure you pay attention to your product's quality as you go. Anything that is low quality or not the right size does not count!

3 When the 3 minutes are up, write down how many of each item you made and add up how much you could make if you sold them, according to the pricing above.

4 What did you learn? Could you have made more by allotting your resources or time differently? If so, try again!

Chocolate bars are made quickly in factories using machines. Each one has to look and taste the same so customers know what to expect. This helps the company save time and money while keeping people happy with the product.

Vocabulary BUILDER
Planning in Action

A production manager oversees how products are made to ensure everything runs smoothly and efficiently. Read these fictional notes from a production manager at a bicycle company to find out how they use demand forecasting to help keep the business on track.

DEMAND FORECASTING NOTES

- This year's sales were up from last year, especially in the spring and summer months when weather was ideal for cycling.
- Warmer weather and longer daylight hours increase demand for both road and mountain bikes.
- The festive season and new year fitness goals often boost interest in bike purchases, especially indoor models.
- Mountain bikes continue to grow in popularity due to off-road cycling trends and more people seeking outdoor activities.
- The road bikes have steady demand, but we have extra inventory – production on these can slow while we focus more on mountain and off-road bikes.
- One of our suppliers has an overstock of off-road tyres – we can get them in bulk at a discounted rate. Buying now could help us prepare for spring demand and increase **profit margins**.

Market	buyers, competition, distribution, launch, pattern, positioning, target
Finance	budget, expenditure, forecast, loss, revenue, sales figures, spending
Stock	availability, product supply, restock, storage, surplus, units, warehouse

Production managers must ensure there are enough goods to meet demand without creating too much waste or extra cost.

Imagine you are the production manager for a popular hot chocolate company. What types of things would you consider when forecasting demand? Use the words in the vocabulary box above and the example on page 42 to write your notes.

- How might the weather affect how many people want hot chocolate?
- What about holidays or winter events?
- What trends might impact your business?

Glossary

Artificial scarcity When the amount of a good or service is intentionally limited so the price can be increased.

Benefit Something good or helpful that you get from something.

Benefit-cost ratio A way to compare what you get (benefit) to what you spend (cost).

Buyer A person who purchases something.

Capital resources Tools, machines and buildings that help people make goods and services.

Cardiology The study of the heart and how to treat heart problems.

Competitive pricing Setting prices based on what others are charging to attract customers.

Consumer A person who uses goods or services, even if they did not buy them themselves.

Deficit A lack of something, such as money or revenue. The opposite of a surplus.

Demand The amount of a good or service that people want and can buy.

Demand-driven scarcity When things become more valuable because there isn't enough to go around (demand is high).

Demand forecasting Trying to predict how much of a product people will want in the future.

Dermatology The study of the skin and how to treat skin problems.

Discounts Lower prices or special deals on products.

Enticing Attractive or appealing.

Equilibrium A balance where supply equals demand.

Expenditure The amount of money that is spent.

Freemium When something is free but you have to pay for extra features.

Housing boom A time when many people are buying homes and prices rise.

Housing market crash A time when fewer people are buying homes and prices fall.

Human resources The people who work in a business.

Imported A product brought in from another country to be sold.

Impulse buy To buy something without planning to.

Incentive Something that encourages someone to do something.

Infrastructure The systems built to support everyday life, such as roads, schools and water systems.

Monopoly When one company controls the whole market for a product or service.

Natural resources Things found in nature that are used to make goods, like water, trees and minerals.

Needs The things we must have to survive, like food, water and shelter.

Oligopoly A market with only a few large companies selling similar products.

Opportunity cost What you give up when you choose one thing over another.

Paediatrics The study of children's health and how to treat their illnesses.

Pioneer A company that is one of the first to explore or develop a new technology or idea, helping to lead change in an industry.

Price reduction A lower price than usual.

Privatised Something that used to be owned and run by the government but is now owned by a private company or person.

Productivity How much work is done in a certain amount of time.

Profit margins The amount of money a business keeps after paying for its costs.

Revenue The total money a business earns before costs are taken out.

Scarcity When there is not enough of something for everyone to get what they want.

Specialisation To focus on doing one thing really well.

Structural scarcity When people can't get what they need – like food or water – even though there is enough. This happens because of problems in the way society is organised.

Subsidies When the government gives money to help people or businesses. This extra money helps lower the cost of things like food, fuel or farming, so people can afford them more easily.

Supply The amount of goods or services available.

Supply-driven scarcity When something costs more because it is hard to find or takes a long time to produce, which makes the supply low.

Surplus An extra amount of something, such as money or revenue. The opposite of a deficit.

Tundra A very cold, dry place where trees cannot grow. Tundras are found near the North Pole and on high mountains.

Vertical integration When a company controls all the steps in making and selling its product, from start to finish.

Wants Things you would like to have but do not need in order to live.

Index

A
Adidas 11
airlines 31
Apple 10
artists 13

B
benefits 22–23
Black Ivory Coffee 35
British Gas Corporation 9
buyers 14–15
Buzz Lightyear figures 34

C
capital resources 6
chocolate bars 41
clothing 17, 18, 31
cocoa 33
coffee 24, 35
competition, business 9, 10–11
consumers 14, 22
control, market 9
corn 30
costs
    and benefits 23
    incentives 25
    opportunity 20–21
Crocs 13

D
De Beers 9
deficit 32
    see also shortage
demand 5, 19
    forecasting 36
    and scarcity 34
diamonds 9, 34
doctors 13
Dubai chocolate 29
Dunkin' 11

E
economics, housing market 38–39
equilibrium 5
expenditure 26

F
farmers 6
fashion 18, 28
fidget spinners 32
Fjällräven 19
focus 12–13
food 16, 18
freemium model 26
Fujifilm 11

G
goals 36–37
government incentives 25

H
housing market 38–39
human resources 6

I
incentives 23, 24–25
income 14, 24

K
Kodak 11

L
Lululemon 7
luxury goods 19

M
manufacturing 13
memory chips 31
milk 30
monopolies 8–9

N
natural resources 6
needs 16–17
Nike 11

O
oligopoly 9
online shopping 7
opportunity costs 20–21
orange juice 33

P
pickleball 33
pistachios 29
popcorn 26
price 4, 5
    and consumers 14
    and demand 19
    and monopolies 8
    and scarcity 34–35
    and shortages 32–33
    and surplus 30
Proctor & Gamble 7
producers 6, 7, 40–41
production managers 42–43
profit 26–27

R
resources 6
revenue 26
RoseArt 29

S
Samsung 10
scarcity 34–35
seasons 14, 37
sellers 6–7
shelter 17
Sherman Antitrust Act 9
shortages 32–33
specialisation 12–13
Standard Oil 9
Starbucks 11
subsidies 25
supermarket points cards 23
supply, defined 4, 5
surplus 30–31
Swift, Taylor 19

T
trade-offs 21
trends 5, 28–29

V
vertical integration 7

W
Walmart 7
wants 18–19
water 16

Acknowledgments

The publisher would like to thank the following for their kind permission to reproduce their photographs:

(Key: a-above; b-below/bottom; c-centre; f-far; l-left; r-right; t-top).

4 Getty Images: Hispanolistic (br); xamtiw (bl). **Getty Images / iStock**: Tim UR (bc). **5 Alamy Stock Photo**: Olena Ivanova (tr). **Getty Images**: RedHelga (c). **6 Getty Images**: Nikola Stojadinovic (bl). **Shutterstock.com**: encierro (cr). **7 Alamy Stock Photo**: SOPA Images Limited (cl). **Getty Images / iStock**: Wolterk (tr). **8 Getty Images / iStock**: welcomia (b). **8-9 Getty Images / iStock**: Sarawut Jaimassiri (bc); Xesai (tc). **9 Getty Images / iStock**: EJ_Rodriquez (crb); HAYKIRDI (cra). **10 Shutterstock.com**: Cincila (bl); Xeniia X (cr); Miguel Lagoa (bc); Mareks Perkons (br). **11 Getty Images / iStock**: FilmColoratStudio (t/Adidas trainer); Wen Sen Tan (t); Watson_images (bl); jfmdesign (bl/Starbucks cup). **Shutterstock.com**: Deutschlandreform (bl/Dunkin cup); isarescheewin (t/Nike trainer). **12 Getty Images**: MTStock Studio (b). **13 Getty Images / iStock**: LarisaBlinova (br). **Shutterstock.com**: DimaBerlin (bl); Hamik (t). **14 Alamy Stock Photo**: Alex Segre (bl). **Getty Images / iStock**: LUNAMARINA (cr); NAKphotos (cr/overlay). **15 Getty Images / iStock**: Jose carlos Cerdeno (tr); Raul_Mellado (cl). **Getty Images**: PeterPencil (tr/overlay). **16-17 Getty Images / iStock**: draganab. **16 Getty Images / iStock**: Madalin Olariu (cr). **Shutterstock.com**: ZinaidaSopina (bl). **17 Alamy Stock Photo**: Patrick Lynch (tl). **Getty Images / iStock**: Sindija Svane (cr). **18-19 Getty Images**: DenisTangneyJr. **18 Alamy Stock Photo**: Antony Nettle (cl). **Getty Images / iStock**: Mariha-kitchen (bc). **19 Alamy Stock Photo**: frantic (c). **Getty Images**: TAS2024 (tl). **20 Getty Images / iStock**: Manuta (t); jiang suying (b). **21 Getty Images / iStock**: Vitalij Sova (t). **Shutterstock.com**: Svet foto (b). **22 Getty Images**: Imgorthand (b). **22-23 Getty Images**: LaylaBird (c). **23 Getty Images**: Maica (cr). **24 Getty Images**: SolStock (b). **Shutterstock.com**: sebra (t). **25 Alamy Stock Photo**: MehmetO (tl); Dinodia Photos (br/overlay). **Getty Images / iStock**: imacoconut (cr); Sviatlana Lazarenka (tl/overlay); zhaojiankang (br). **26 Alamy Stock Photo**: Danny Hooks (b). **Getty Images**: Goodboy Picture Company (t). **27 Getty Images / iStock**: BreakingTheWalls (bc); Ekaterina Zvonko (br). **Shutterstock.com**: Laguna781 (tr); seramo (cl). **28 Alamy Stock Photo**: Lou-Foto (bl). **28-29 Getty Images / iStock**: aldomurillo (bc); MurzikNata (tc). **29 Getty Images / iStock**: art-4-art (crb); NoDerog (cra). **30 Getty Images / iStock**: ghornephoto (t); jenifoto (b). **31 Alamy Stock Photo**: Jens Metschurat (b). **Shutterstock.com**: Natali Kuzina (t). **32 Shutterstock.com**: MNStudio (b). **33 Getty Images**: magnetcreative (bl). **Getty Images / iStock**: Unaihuiziphotography (t). **Shutterstock.com**: DenisNata (cl). **34 Alamy Stock Photo**: Phanuwat Nandee (tr). **35 Alamy Stock Photo**: Przemysaw Nieprzecki (bl). **Shutterstock.com**: Wirestock Creators (background). **36-37 Getty Images**: imaginima. **36 Getty Images / iStock**: coldsnowstorm (bl); Prykhodov (br). **37 Getty Images / iStock**: BartekSzewczyk (cb); panpote (tr). **Getty Images**: SolStock (tl). **38 Alamy Stock Photo**: Connect Images (clb). **Getty Images / iStock**: JohnnyH5 (cr). **Shutterstock.com**: PeopleImages.com - Yuri A (br). **39 Alamy Stock Photo**: MBI (t). **Getty Images / iStock**: Feverpitched (b/overlay); Konoplytska (b). **40 Getty Images / iStock**: Artem Stepanov. **41 Getty Images / iStock**: Евгений Хабаров (br). **43 Getty Images**: whitebalance.space

Cover images: *Front:* **Dreamstime.com**: Oskanov br; **Shutterstock.com**: GreenOak bl, industryviews cr, Linda_288 t; *Back:* **Alamy Stock Photo**: Olena Ivanova t; **Getty Images / iStock**: Xesai b; **Shutterstock.com**: Natali Kuzina c.